BUDGETING THROUGH GOD'S WORD

By: Claudette A Scales

Published by CAS publications

P.O. Box 365

Henderson, NC 27536

ISBN 978-1-304-99577-3

Acknowledgement

This book is dedicated through the Holy Spirit for inspiring its writing.

Thank you to the following for their continued support and encouragement: Marciano Scales (husband); Shelomon Scales (son), Bobbie J. Lowe (sister), and Shirley Clark (dear friend). Recognition is given to the late Elizabeth Waddell Monroe for encouraging the use of budgeting, and encouraging me to write it.

Disclaimer

Chapters

Chapter I- Budget Discipline

Chapter II- Christian Principles for Budgeting

Chapter III- Role of Visions in Budgeting

Chapter IV- Budgeting the Cost of Credit

Chapter V- Tithing

Chapter VI- Setting Up A Budget Ledger

Chapter VII- I Don't Have Enough Money

Chapter VIII- Budgeting With a Spouse

Chapter IX- Just My Opinion

Chapter X—Finding Money in Your Budget

Acknowledgements

Introduction

The inspiration to write <u>Budgeting Through God's Word</u> was motivated from frustration with personal debt, and the observation of Christians struggling with debt, unpaid bills, and creditors.

The intent of this book is to encourage discipline as a way to get out of debt and gain control in financial areas. It is not a quick fix, but a way to be in control of your personal finances; as well as, enhancing the ability to communicate effectively with creditors.

This book tells us that we need more than financial information. We need to follow God's Word as we practice discipline. We need to develop vision plans.

Unlike other materials on finances and budgeting, the focus is on practicing until budgeting becomes an enjoyable task that reaps many blessings.

Chapter I
Budget Discipline

Budgeting begins with discipline. Budget discipline is defined as "the ability to make oneself live within the finances available". It is the recognition of what one has to spend and self-control in staying within that spending limit. This is not to say that we will always have the same spending limits, but like driving we'll know when to accelerate and when to decelerate. Our discipline will give us spending limits.

Why discipline with budgeting?

Overspending is like trying to wear a size 6 shoe when we know we wear a size 9. Sooner or later something is going to ache. Discipline with budgeting helps us avoid the aches and pains created from squeezing and stretching into the wrong size. It gives us freedom to make more choices about our lives.

Discipline helps in other ways as well. When we appear to have extra money, the lender wants to give us more in exchange for it with fees. Without discipline, we blindly accept the offer; then, fees overtake what we had to start with. In addition, the givers stop giving, but continue to take from us through interest, fees, and often harassing phone calls. Budget discipline puts this in check. It allows us to be in control. When followed consistently, it eliminates living paycheck to paycheck, harassing phone calls from creditors, while encouraging wise use of money.

An Eye Opener

Just as satan convinced Eve that the appointed fruit in the garden was not adequate, he is still convincing Christians that their needs are not met (Gen.:1-6). In short, he says, "what God has supplied is not adequate, you can really have more right now, it won't kill you."

Dave Branon sums our attitudes up well in an article entitled "Gotta Have It." He writes, "I keep seeing the car I want. It's not the same care all the time, you understand. Yesterday, it was a showroom new-looking Ford Explorer that was proudly displaying a "for sale" sign. A few weeks back it was a shiny blue Cavalier. Other times a nice red jeep seems mighty inviting. Of course, when you're driving a rusty, gray Horizon that's been a third of the way to the moon…you can feel justified in looking for a replacement. The problem is, like everyone else, I've learned to be dissatisfied with the functional. After the entire Horizon still works… Yet, here's how we think: If our coat keeps us warm, it's not good enough unless it's the latest style…. If our shoes have traction and they support our ankles as we play ball, they are headed for oblivion if they aren't advertised by…."

Budgeting opens our eyes to the truth of how much we actually have to spend, when to spend it, and where to spend it.

Budget discipline dispels coveting. As we develop discipline with budgeting, we learn when we are coveting in the financial areas.

"And he said unto them, Take heed, and beware of covetousness: for a man's life consisteth not in the abundance of the things which he possesseth:" (Luke 12:15)

Often we measure our accomplishments through physical eyes instead of spiritual eyes. As a result, coveting develops subtly when discipline is not used.

We live in a society where we bring various pay amounts home from the same job simply because taxes, insurances, and pay options vary. Yet, we continue to set our standards by others.

Let's use Cary and Charlie for example. Cary earns ten dollars an hour, works 40 hours a week, is in the 20% tax bracket. He chose standard option insurance, has four dependents. Charles earns ten dollars an hour, works 40 hours a week. He is in the 20% tax bracket, has four dependents, but chose the high option insurance, has five dollars per paycheck deducted for a savings bond in his oldest child's name, and five dollars sent to Unicef per pay period. Both have identical withholdings for federal, state, etc. purposes. Who probably brings home the most money in net pay?

Charlie sees Cary buying new living room furniture for his house and decides he should update his furniture as well. Charlie is probably making a mistake. Cary has more net money to work with for purchases. He pays less in insurance, has controllable charitable contributions, does not have bonds taken out before his net pay. However, satan deceives us into believing that we should be so much alike that we are financially the same as our friends.

When was the last time you sat in casual conversation with a friend and asked, "So are you changing your withholdings this year?" What will you have deducted from your pay this month?" Yet, we observe others and decide that our cars, houses, clothes, etc. are not adequate by the standards of what others have. Budget discipline keeps this type of coveting in check as it shows physically what we have financially.

Discipline helps in another area of coveting as well. Often, we covet people in another salary scale. We've often heard the quote: "the more you make, the more it takes." My sister clarified this statement for me one day. She said, "As people earn more money, they tend to live at higher standards." Trying to keep up with someone on a higher salary scale is not only stressful, but ignorant; unless, you have learned how to obtain wealth by other means.

The best way to understand this is to compare money in percentages. Ten percent of one hundred is ten. Ten percent of two hundred is twenty. If I net $100 and can absolutely spend only ten percent in anything I want, I can spend $10. If you net $200 and can absolutely spend only ten percent in anything you want, you can only spend $20. I cannot spend the $20 that you spent if I only have ten percent to spare because you simply have more money than I do. Without discipline I could go ahead and spend the same amount as you. But spending that extra $10 will cause me to squeeze into that size six, while another need goes lacking.

However, with discipline, one can develop good spending habits and can eventually have more spending money than a person with a higher salary but poor spending habits.

Chapter II
Christian Principles for Budgeting

Does God really set forth principles for finances?

Budgeting Through God's Word is encouraged from biblical instruction that teaches us the need for knowledge, understanding, and wisdom. We may not think of finances and biblical knowledge, understanding, and wisdom together, but biblical knowledge, understanding, and wisdom implemented with discipline can develop and strengthen financial areas.

The book of Proverbs teaches us much on the importance of knowledge, wisdom, and understanding in life.

"Through wisdom a house is builded: and by understanding it is established: and by knowledge shall the chambers be filled with precious and pleasant riches."
(Prov 24:3-4)

"The heart of the prudent getteth knowledge; and the ear of the wise seeketh knowledge." (Prov 18:15)

"Wisdom is the principal thing; therefore get wisdom: and with all thy getting get understanding..." (Prov 4:7)

Godly principles, **knowledge** of real moneys available; clear **understanding** of financial areas; and **wisdom** in the use of money will help us manage money as God intended. We do not need to rely on unrighteous behavior to achieve financial freedom. God's Word instructs us in how to obtain blessings and riches in the financial areas, and gives us specific knowledge about financial areas.

What about repaying debts?

Psalm 37:21 tells us that the "wicked borroweth, and payeth not again; but the righteous showeth mercy and giveth."

Principle: God desires that we repay our obligations and be able to give to others. Do we want to be classified as wicked because we borrow and are not disciplined enough to repay? If repaying is not important to God, He would not have included it for our information.

Are credit records important?

"A good name is rather to be chosen than great riches, and loving favour rather than silver and gold" (Prov 22:1)

Principle: Our credit record should be good. In this century our credit record continues to be a portrayal of our name to many who will never see us.

Should we have savings, budgets, and investments?

"There is treasure to be desired and oil in the dwelling of the wise: but a foolish man spendeth it up." (Prov 21:20)

Principle: We are to be wise in how we use and spend our money. It should not all disappear quickly. We should have something to show for our labor.

Are we to borrow money?

"The rich ruleth over the poor, and the borrower is servant to the lender." (Prov 22: 7)

Principle: We should be in a position to lend money, goods, etc.; otherwise accept that we are the servant to another.

Does God want us to work?

The Word of God is full of scriptures on working people and the need to work.

"Go to the ant, thou sluggard: consider her ways and be wise: which having no guide, overseer, or ruler, provided her meat in the summer, and gather her food in the harvest…" (Prov 6:6-8)

"But if any provide not for his own, and specially for those of his own house, he hath denied the faith and is worse than an infidel." (I Timothy 5:8)

"I went by the field of the slothful and by the vineyard of the man void of understanding; and, lo, it was all grown over with thorns, and nettles had covered the face thereof, and the stone wall thereof was broken. Then I saw, and considered well: I looked upon it, and received instruction. Yet a little sleep, a little slumber, a little folding of the hands to sleep; so shall thy poverty come as one that travelleth: and thy want as an armed man. "(Prov 24:30-34)

Principle: Slothfulness brings on poverty. God wants us to work to provide for our needs, and the needs of our family.

Am I suppose to give every time someone asks me to?

"Be not thou one of them that strike hands, or of them that are sureties for debts, if thou has nothing to pay, why should he take away thy bed from thee?"
(Prov 22: 26-27)

Principle: Use wisdom in where to give, who to give to, and how much to give. Is it wise to agree to pay another's debt, knowing you have not paid your own? Often, we know that we haven't enough to give, yet we give knowing that we're giving away what we have contracted or promised to another.

Note that tithing is not giving away. It is one of the areas you owe in anyway.

We can quote a variety of Scriptures to support giving or not giving. The Word of God says to "study to show thyself approved, **unto God**", a workman that need not be ashamed"... (II Timothy 2:15). We must study to see if the scripture is talking about the character of the giver or the act of giving.

God's Word clearly indicates that giving is important in the Christian's life.

However, it is very important to pray and know that God is speaking directly to you when hearing instructions to give. It is the same idea as marriage. If someone else has to tell you to do it before you hear it from God, then it is questionable. If it's already in your spirit or a confirmation, then you know the answer. Remember God does not make us feel guilty nor does He leave us lacking. If your spirit tells you to give, then God has already made a way for you to receive more. If you continually give and feel guilty later because you cannot meet other obligations, then seek God for the truth about your personal giving. You may be listening to man and not God.

How important is financial gain?

"Riches profit not in the day of wrath: but righteousness delivereth from death" (Prov 11:4)

"For the love of money is the root of all evil: which while some coveted after, they have erred from the faith, and pierced themselves through with many sorrows."
(I Timothy 6:10)

"A faithful man shall abound with blessings: but he that maketh haste to be rich shall not be innocent."
(Prov 28:20)

"Thus saith the Lord, let not the wise man glory in his wisdom…let not the rich man glory in his riches: but let him that glorieth glory in this, that he, understandeth and knoweth me…
(Jeremiah 9:23-24)

Principle: We are not to become so involved in laboring for riches that we forget God. When we forget God we create negative consequences.

Wise budgeting brings about wealth. Whether or not we keep the wealth depends on our management skills.

Remember : "Seek ye first the kingdom of God…" (Matt 6:33)

Chapter III
Visions are important

Effective budgeting requires a vision plan, because visions encourage the discipline needed to budget as indicated in proverbs, "For without a vision people perish."

Having a vision encourages us to set aside moneys and to keep track of where our moneys are going. It is not to be confused with daydreaming of wishing. It is an actual plan that can be worked towards and made to come to past.

Webster dictionary defines a vision as "an act or sense of seeing." Vine dictionary defines the Greek word vision (optasia): "to see, a coming into view…"

In 1997 Bishop Don Mears summed up the importance of visions in his sermon, Dare to be a Line Crosser. He profoundly says: "You've got to have a vision or else you will perish. You got to have a dream, something that will motivate you to sacrifice, to give up something today for what you are going to receive tomorrow. …Give people a dream, a vision, destiny that gives them hope…a reason. With it there'' be times of difficulty that comes in our life and the result is we're gonna quit, but with … a vision…then we will always go through whatever we'll going through."

His message is especially true of finances. Why should we save for tomorrow if we have no hopes and plans for tomorrow?

With a vision, our finances come alive! We look forward to what we will have tomorrow because of our budget plan. We begin to decide if the latest shoes are more important than bonds for college. Should we save for a house or buy the latest model car?

Visions take a series of steps instead of materializing immediately. It is important to put the vision on paper and work it into the budget. We need to list ways to obtain the moneys needed. It may be through savings accounts, direct deductions from pay, planner's clubs, layaway, etc.

Visions encourage us to begin to take actions steps; such as, research information on what we want. If the vision is to invest in bonds, then we need to read articles on different types and companies. If the vision is to purchase a house, we may need to make decisions on the type or where we want to look. How much can we afford in mortgage payments? How will we save for the down payment and fees?

The more we put into our vision, the more likely we are to strive to achieve it. We must heed the advice in James, "…Being a hearer of the word and not a doer; he is like unto a man beholding his natural face in a glass: for he beholdeth himself and goeth his way, and straightway forgetteth what manner of man he was." (James 1:23-24)

It is just as easy to forget what manner of vision we had, or how we planned to accomplish it once we have finished thinking about it; therefore, visions must be written down.

They should include a list of the following:
-**How long do I want to take to get it**?
-**What do I need to do to obtain the vision?**

Be very specific with the vision plan.

Chapter IV
Budgeting the Cost of Money

The purpose of this chapter is to encourage you to determine your own monthly finance charges and to practice lowering them through knowledge.

How nice it would be if every seventh year we could forgive or be forgiven of debt. If only interest on old debt was forgiven many of us would be much wealthier.

Finance companies, banks, loan organizations, etc. stay in business based on our interest. The actual interest charged us is what keeps the companies in business. By the same means we could be in our own business if we learn to manage our personal interest or to keep the interest in our possessions. We can really eliminate the notion that we are making another rich while we get poorer.

Understanding the basics of how interest works will help with a realistic budget.

Consistently using the formula for calculating your monthly interest against payments will encourage better spending habits. We can also track the cost of spending.

Many bills include a section that tells how much money you will have spent if you pay only the minimum amount. Read it. Decide what you need to do to pay off the bill as early as possible.

Two basic steps will help with learning the effect of interest on bills.

Step 1: Get in the habit of always looking at the interest calculations on the bill.

Step 2: Pay close attention to the following areas: balance subject to finance charge, daily periodic rate, corresponding percentage rate, periodic finance charge, previous balance and current balance.

The key is to continually practice plugging in the numbers until you feel comfortable with it.

We shall review the use of our finance charge language in layman's terms, then work with the formulas.

Finance charge: extra money you pay for borrowing or using another's money.

Annual finance charge: amount of money you agreed the company could charge you per year for use of the money when accepted loan contract.

Monthly periodic rate: amount of finance charge calculated by dividing the annual finance rate by 12. For example, the annual finance charge of 21.90% divided by 12 equals **1.825** (monthly rate)

Daily periodic rate: amount of finance charge you owe each day on a debt: calculated by dividing the monthly periodic rate by days that the company bills you, usually 30 or 31.

An example: On an annual periodic rate of 21.90 percent the daily periodic rate for 31 days would be

1.825/31= 0.0588709 (rate you're billed each day.) Of course you can round the amount off to .059.

Payments/credits: amounts paid or given to your account, hopefully decreasing the balance owed.

Previous balance: exactly as implied, the previous balance before credits or debits (refers to last month's balance in our scenarios)

New balance: will refer to anticipated balance that finance charges will add to or payments will subtract from (usually listed as balance subject to finance charges)

The formula used in determining how interest is added to your bill should be explained on the bill somewhere (usually on the back of the bill).

Read closely as we go through 3 steps in calculating interest on one bill.
The steps are:

Step 1: Multiply the balance subject to finance charges (balances due) by the daily periodic rate in %

_____X _____(%) = _____
(balance)   (daily rate)   (cents owed)

Step 2: Multiply that amount by the number of days listed in your billing cycle (remember each day you owe this amount)

$$\underline{\qquad\qquad} \times \underline{\qquad\qquad} = \underline{\qquad\qquad}$$
(cents owed)   (30, 31,etc)   (monthly amt)
Step 3: The total should be the listed finance charge
on your bill or close to it.

****If two different methods or rates are listed on
your bill, you need to do both, then add them to get
the finance charge***

Our example is from a bill that is $1086.33

Balance subject to finance charges is 1086.33 on
method A

The annual percentage rate is 20.49.
The daily periodic rate is 0.0550806%.
The billing cycle equals 31 days.

Step 1: $\underline{1086.33}$ X $\underline{0.0550806\%}$ = $\underline{0.598357}$
         balance   daily rate   cents owed

Step 2: $\underline{0.598357}$ X $\underline{31}$ = $\underline{18.549067}$
         daily cost   days = monthly cost

18.549067 Or $18.55 is the current finance charge
for the month unless another rate or method is
added.

Let's pretend that another method is used on the
bill.
    Jull still owes $800.00 for credit card cash that
was withdrawn from the automatic teller on this
same bill. This amount shows up on the line

beneath regular purchases as cash advances with interest, fees included as $881.24.

The daily rate is 0.0550806%

Step 1: $\underline{\$881.24}$ x $\underline{0.0550806}$ = $\underline{0.4853922}$
       balance   daily rate   cost

Step 2: $\underline{0.4853922}$ x $\underline{31}$ = $\underline{15.047158}$
      daily cost   days   monthly rate

The finance charge for this bill is now the first calculation of $18.549067 + 15.047158, which equals 33.596225 or 33.60.

You now know that out of any moneys paid, the company keeps $33.60 as interest.

Now you can decide if you want to spend that extra $40.00 eating out or put part or all of the $40.00 aside to extra on the bill.

What's the purpose of tracking finance charges?

The more money you add to the bill, the less your balance will be; thereby, reducing your daily balance and total finance charges paid. You will pay the bill off quicker. For example if you add the additional $40.00 to the amount the company will bill you anyway, you'll pay the bill off sooner.

Here's a story of three families with the same identical bill as listed above. The balance is $1086.33 for charges plus $881.24 for cash withdrawals. The total bill is 1,967.57. We know that the finance charge this month is $33.60. *the minimum payment due should be $33.60.

Family 1: The King family pays $33.60 on their bill each month.

Family 2: The Casey family pays $38.60 instead of $33.60

Family 3: The Vicks pay $43.60 each month instead of 33.60.

This is what happened to their bills:

The Kings did not make any decreases in the balance. In a few months they will owe more because finance charges will keeping adding to the amount they owe. In fact, most likely, they will eventually have no credit available on the account, even if they don't purchase on it; unless the company increases the available limit.

The Caseys did make a decrease of $5.00 in the debt. If they continue over a period of time, the extra $5.00 will equal more because it causes the interest to be less if the account is not used.

The Vicks made a larger decrease than the others. They made a dent of $10.00. They will also make a larger decrease in the bill in a shorter period of time unless they start to purchase on the account and increase the amount owed.

Paying more than the required minimum payment will add money to your budget eventually when it eliminates that bill from your budget.

Suppose you have 6 bills listed on your budget. Think about this: How much money would you have if you only had 5 bills? How much money would you have if you could eliminate a car payment or credit card sooner?

Check your bills to see if some of the payment goes into the actual balance due and some into interest owed the company. Even then paying more will help eliminate the bill sooner. Remember, bills never seem to decrease when the company only bill for the finance charge due them.

Let's suppose we want to pay a bill off in twelve months or less. The steps are the same. However, we must add enough extra money to the bill to eliminate it. For example, in the case of the 1,967.57 bill, approximately 164.00 must be added each month to eliminate the bill in twelve months. *remember the interest will be less each month when more is paid*

Eliminating the higher finance rate first is not necessarily the best method. For example, you have $50.00 extra to add to a bill each month. Let's say you are paying 120.00 on a $500.00 balance at 15.98% interest rate and you are paying $50.00 on $2000.00 balance at 17.595 interest rate, which you'd like to pay off. You may think about putting the extra money on the $2000.00. However, you may want to add the extra $50 to the $120 payment; thereby, paying it off in approximately 2.5 payments. You can then add the $50 and the $120.00 toward the $2000 or add the $120.00 and still have $50.00 to add towards your vision plan.

How special offers affect your bills

"You're a good customer, Skip a payment plan"

Or

"Your credit's so good "buy now", no payments until next year", "Deferred Payments"

Often, companies will offer the good customer, skip a month payment, or buy now-pay later plans. Oh, how wonderful! But what happened to the interest? The interest does not stop adding up just because you are exempted from payment. Read the contract. According to our agreement with the lender, the interest is still due, but will be added to the next month's balance until payments start. In short, this doubles our interest; thereby, giving more money to the lender.

There is usually a statement indicating that charges start at a specific date (usually date or purchase) written on the offer for deferments unless payment is made in full.

On the 1967.57 debt, the $33.60 was added to the 1967.57 the month we skipped a payment. Our balance is now $1967.57 = $33.60 or $2001.17 plus interest for the paying month.

The same occurs if we do not make a payment for 6 or twelve months. If we sign an agreement that includes monthly finance charges, then the finance charge is added monthly and we'll see it when we start paying on the bill. After twelve months our $1965.57 bill will be an estimated $2370.77 or ($33.60 x 12 = 403.20) – 1967.57.

If the agreement is **no interest due** for twelve months, then the interest should not be added for twelve months, but it may show up later. If the agreement is **no interest charged** for twelve months, then no amount should be added to the bill monthly, until after the twelve month period. Ensure you understand the language of the contract, when your interest starts, and how it will be calculated when it starts.

It feels good to be rewarded for paying bills on time and being honest. But over a period of time this is one feeling that we pay for. Remember, lenders, banks, loan organizations are motivated by the need to get more money to stay in business. Have you ever noticed how we're usually rewarded at the most tempting times: holiday seasons, tax times, and vacation seasons? Skipping payments, and delayed payments have the same effect as late payments but without the negative credit rating or late payment fees.

Indeed a service is provided, but a service that you are paying for with extra interest charges, unless you can pay the bill in full.

Eliminate the interest on the late fees by paying on time. Think of late fees as free extra money and interest to the company. Always pay the late fee if a bill is not paid on time. Otherwise you'll pay interest on that same late fee over and over. If you have a late fee of $25; an over the limit fee of $25 on the bill that was 1965.57, you now owe 1967.57+25+25 which equals 2017.57 x the interest rate.

Chapter V
Tithes and Offerings

I hesitated to include a chapter on tithing because it is a controversial area for Christians and non-Christians. This chapter is included because tithing and offerings are beneficial to Christians and non-Christians. Please read it knowing that it's an area of choice from God.

Because satan is well versed in Biblical Scriptures and is determined to defeat God's people (Ephesians 6:12)" **for we fight not against flesh and blood...",** tithing is often a very difficult area for Christians to start and maintain. Christians must remember that just as if satan had known the end results of Jesus's crucifixion, he would have tried to prevent it, he knows the end result of tithing and therefore has a strong force against tithing. (I Corinthians 2:8) "which none of the princes of this world knew: for had they known it, they would not have crucified the Lord of glory".

Satan knows the results of tithing because he knows the Scriptures. He knows the power in the scripture.

The subject of tithing creates much discussion and controversy. Tithing however, is encouraged in budgeting because despite all, the Word of God teaches tithing with a promise to be taken care of. "Let us therefore fear, lest a promise being left us of entering into his rest, any of you should seem to come short of it..." (Hebrews 4:1-2)

"Bring ye all the tithes into the storehouse, that there may be meat in mine house, and prove me now herewith, saith the Lord of hosts, if I will not open you the windows of heaven, and pour you out a blessing, that there shall not be room enough to receive it…" (Malachi 3:10-12)

I believe that we should put on the whole armor of God. For it is better to have armor and never need it, than to need armor and not have any. In short, it is better to try God's Word for the benefit than to never try it.

Many excuses are used for not tithing. The famous ones are that the church "doesn't spend the money appropriately"; the leaders are wealthy and the people are poor." Tithing was for the Mosaic days."

My response is that God did not say that our rewards would come from how the people in authority use the tithing but from the integrity in His Word. If ever there was time when people in general need the benefits of tithing, it is in these modern days when inflation has taken over and the value of the dollar is less. We work long hours for less pay.

God knew as much about this day when the Holy books were written as He knew about the day on which they were written. Surely, He would have put in place another plan to keep the enemy from devouring our finances, handiwork, blessings, etc. if He had not already put the perfect plan in place.

I personally prefer not to discuss tithing. It brings taxation to mind. I favor tithing over taxes because I am given a choice. I favor tithing because it is less than the governmental rule of taking. I've had as much as 40% taken from paychecks in taxes. No one asked me if I wanted to give 40% to governmental agencies. They just took it. Even worse, there wasn't a list to check off what storehouse I'd like that 40% to go into. In fact, even my retirement amount is chosen without my approval. Furthermore, I don't agree with one-half of how the taxes are spent; so how, can I justify not paying tithes based on my opinion of how they are used. Also, finance companies get free money from us (my opinion). I pay them faithfully each month what I borrowed, plus interest; however, if I'm late one minute pass the due date, I am assessed an additional fee, called a "late fee. God does not assess me a late fee. His mercy is renewed daily. His mercy and loving kindness extends from generation to generation.

Granted like other things in our society, tithing paid to a ministry can be abused and misused; but I will not suffer because of it. I will get the benefits that God says I will get for paying my tithes.

I myself can be accused of feeling that the storehouse did not adequately meet someone's needs. (Of course, I don't know the whole story). Just as I've disagreed with the use of tithing, I've also witnessed the benefits of tithing in my life and the life of family and friends. I thank God that He does not reward us according to what others do, but according to obedience to His plan and promises. The Scriptures teach us that **"God is not a man, that He should lie nor the son of man that He should repent: hath he not said it, and shall He not do it…?" (Numbers 23:19)**

Luke 6:38 teaches that "give and it shall be given unto you: good measure, pressed down, and shaken together, and running over, shall men give into your bosom. For with the same measure that you mete withal it shall be measured to you again."

One striking aspect of tithing is in Malachi 3:11 "… and I will rebuke the devourer for your sakes, and he shall not destroy the fruits of your ground; neither shall your vine cast her fruit before the time in the field…"

We know that the devourer is satan. He makes sure that we see the devouring in the physical realm; so that, we do not credit it with spiritual warfare. We tend to say "this happened and that happened." We could list many areas in the physical realm where occurrences can wipe out finances: medical bills, vehicle repairs, tuition, etc. In the tithing arena, we need to know that if we tithe with money, then satan is unable to destroy in an area that will affect our finances.

We must also be aware that sometimes satan does not directly devour our finances, but when God blesses us, we choose to give our finances away. The Word of God says cast not your pearls to the swine (Matt: 7:6). An example is constantly giving money in a area you do not have to give it in, i.e. lottery, spending money at locations that are set up to take our money without providing an equal service. God gives the increase, but our finances are trampled. God continues to bless us, but we continue to see the blessing devoured because of the choices we're making. What about people we give to? I am not saying that one should stop giving to loved ones? Are we making a positive impact on the person's life with our financial giving? Would it be better to give in a manner that will help the person get out of the situation, or on towards financial stability?

Satan hopes that the more he devours, the less meat there will be in the storehouse. If the storehouses are not supported, fewer gospel will spread. Satan is hoping that fewer people will be saved, more will be in hell with him; hereby hurting God, which is his ultimate goal.

Let's suppose we go shopping. We leave the house with $100. On the way, a pick pocketer steals $50. Upon entering the cashier line, we check our pockets and discover $50 is missing. Can we spend $100? Unless God intervenes, we will only be able to get $50 worth of items. This is especially true in the church. If satan picks pockets before we get to the church, he thinks there will be less for the church. But God has promised, He will "rebuke" not destroy, the devourer for us. Rebuke is defined as "prevent" in some internationals versions of the Holy Bible. Webster refers to rebuke as "to force back."

God has many ways of rebuking the devourer for us and many ways of meeting our needs when we are in line with His Word. His Word tells us that our ways are not His ways, His thoughts are not our thoughts: **(Isaiah 55:8);** therefore we must learn to hear what God is saying to us in the areas of tithing and blessings.

Financial blessings should not be defined as winning a million dollar lottery. God may not be thinking to directly bless with specific moneys. But what He blesses us with may generate money. Many people become millionaires with a single thought, and endurance, but little or no money.

In the same manner, we must not think that we will solve all ills and problems with tithing. Disease, hunger, marital problems will be solved according to the whole Word of God.   Therefore let us hear the voice of God and act accordingly when it comes to tithing and budgeting.

Offerings are separate from tithing. They are given after tithing and as we purpose in our hearts, cheerfully, with God rewarding us for our act of giving. **(II Corinthian 9: 1-15)**

Paul clearly explains why he asked for offerings from the Christians. He encourages their giving by assuring them that it will be God who will reward them for generosity **(vs. 8).** He goes on to explain that the offering will minister to the saints **(vs. 12).** The amplified version of **vs. 7** states… **"whose heart is in his giving".** I point this out because to be a cheerful giver we must believe in the purpose for which we are giving. It is much easier to give an offering to a building fund when we believe that God's house should represent Him (glorious and adequate for those inside it.) It is easier to give cheerfully to an offering for Christian education when we believe that children need a Christian education.

Unlike tithing (one-tenth), offering is given as one purpose in his heart. We often misquote **Malachi 3** with "bring all the tithes and offerings to the storehouse. **Malachi 3:8** states that God has been robbed "…**In tithes and offerings."** Verse 10 states **"bring ye all the tithes into the storehouse…"**

We often mix the two- justifying not paying tithing by defining it as an offering or not paying an offering because we have paid tithing. Clearly they are separated as God uses both words in verse 8. Verse 8 indicates that we can rob God of either or both.

I suggest amidst the conversations and teachings about tithing and offering study and pray: **"Lest satan should get an advantage of us: for we are not ignorant of his devices."**
II Corinthians 2:11

"Honour the Lord with thy substance, and with the first fruits of all thine increase: so shall thy barns be filled with plenty, and thy presses shall burst out with new wine". (Prov 3: 9-10)

Chapter VI
Creating and Setting Up a Personal Budget Ledger

This section is for persons who want to develop their own written budget. There are many electronic budgets available for free or a fee. I recommend that you use the manual budget if you are new to budgeting or just getting started. Technology is mentioned later.

If you are using paper bills/notices, you should read the information in the envelope. If using electronic bills you can read, then copy and save your information to a personal folder on your computer.

A few preliminary steps are necessary before starting the actual paper manual budget.

1. Purchase a six or more column ledger/ or analysis pad (not a worded budget book. Purchase a color that is attractive to you. Stores that carry office supplies may offer a variety of colors and types. I started with a colorful theme tablet with the vertical lines drawn in.
2. Set aside a quiet place, day and time when you will work on your ledger, at least 30 minutes, twice a month, even if you get paid monthly. (One day should be a day or two before your payday)

3. Place all bills in an inexpensive caddy; file box, letter holder, etc. as soon as you get them. ***Never leave bills lying on counters, tables, desks, etc. ***   Later as you practice budgeting, you will remember the due dates and determine the amount to pay; therefore, you may not need to open the bill until you sit down to work on your ledger.

4. Place the ledger in a convenient place

5. Always read the terms and conditions papers in the bill envelope. As indicated in the finance chapter, they affect your payments and total cost. Save term and condition papers.

6. Put your vision at the top of the ledger. Remember visions take a series of steps. With discipline, self control and consistent budgeting you will achieve your vision goal.

7. Discard all advertisements inside the bills immediately upon opening them. They will make budgeting tedious and possibly increase debt. Many of the items advertised are sold directly from a local store or mail order catalog. If you didn't notice that you need the item before opening the envelope, then you probably don't need it anyway.

Steps to completing an individual budget

Using the following steps, fill in your attractive budget ledger. *Review the attached sample pages before completing your ledger, then go back and review each step as you do your own ledger*

Sample budgets: The Following example budget pages show two different ways that I've budgeted payments for the following bills. One budget reflects that I was able to make some payments in April for May. The other budgets shows only May monies used.

Financial Obligations (weekly or monthly)
Paycheck amount $550 each week.

Tithing: 10%	$220	Car gas:	$20
Associate	$50	Electric bill	$100
First Union	$600	Master charge	$38
Auto Insurance	$200	Savings	$80
Auto Loan	$200	Water Bill	$50
Groceries	$325	Heat Bill	$75

Sample: This is what step 1 should look like for a budget from May 0000

The month is May. The pay dates are the 7th, 14th, 21, and 28th. The estimated paycheck amount is $550.00 each payday.

<u>May 0000</u>

<u>Pay dates: 7   14   21   28</u>
          550.00   550.00   550.00 550.00
Amount due   amount due amount due amount due

The following steps are based on a six column
ledger and receiving a paycheck each week. Once a
month and bi-weekly paycheck ledgers are
explained later.

Step 1- At the top of the ledger page; write the
current month and year in.

1a- Below the month/year write in the word "Pay
Dates" on the left, but leave at least three blank
columns to the left for the next step.

1b- Across from the "pay dates" write the actual
pay dates putting one in each column.

1c- On the next row, below the words pay dates
write in the estimated paycheck amount. (It's okay
if you have flexible amounts in your paycheck). As
you budget, you will learn how to manage and
control flexible pay amounts. It is important that
you be honest with yourself in the amount you
estimate in your paycheck.

1d- On the next row below paycheck amount write
in the words amount due for the amount that is due.

Step 2- Complete the left two columns that were left blank. In the first column on the same row as the amount due put in the words or initials "date due/paid". In the next column write in the words or initials "Bills/balance".

Step 2a- Under the bill/balance column; list all current bills and the balance on the bills. Include anticipated expenditures; such as, mother's day gifts or Memorial Day activity costs. Remember the balance is from the financial summary sections of the bill.
Writing the balance will help you track the increase or decrease in the bill. You will also notice quicker if there is a discrepancy on your bill.

Step 2b- Under the date due write the pay by the date from the bill. Many companies have a set date. The actual paid date column will be filled in when you pay the bill.

Your ledger should look like this now:

May 0000						
Paydates:			7	14	21	22
Pay check amt			550	550	550	550
Datedue	bd	billsbalance		amt due		
5-2		Associate Bank/2300		50.		
5-1		First Union/7500		600.		
5-18		Mastercharge//4000		38.		
5-1		Allstate/658		200		

Step 3 you are now ready to plan your actual budget for the month. At this step you will decide the amount due and when to pay it.

3a- Looking at the due date, fill in the amounts due to match a pay date so that the bill is not paid late, yet not so early that you are taking money from your vision plan. *every bill should have a pay date or two. There should be no blank "bill listed" columns for this budget.

Steps 4- At the bottom of each pay date column subtract the moneys paid out from the paycheck amount. This is your balance. Put + to indicate extra money or a – to indicate not enough money on that date. This will help you know where to adjust or move money around. It helps to write in total amount paid out and total balance left.

   Note that after you fulfill your financial obligations you can decide what to do with any + moneys. You can add them to your vision plan, treat yourself, etc. We will discuss negative balances in Chapter VII.

Step5- After you practice budgeting for a month or two, you may begin to work ahead a month. For example, I have noticed in April that June's summer camp will be $100. I'll add this amount to May and June's page ledger. As June approaches I can evaluate my finances and decide if I'll actually spend the $100 on summer camp or look for other alternatives.

   First Union is due May 1st. The Allstate is due May 1st also, in addition to my tithing, food and gas in the same week. I must make a sound decision with the money available. Something should have been saved from April for May 1st in order for me to stay ahead. *Do not send the payment a month ahead because the creditor may not credit it as payment for the next month. For example, Associates may accept your May payment in April but still expect you to pay another payment in May* Get the money order, check, etc. completed for May but do not send it until the appropriate time.

You may think "but April is gone!" This is why it is important to start a budget as soon as possible. It is important to work the next month into the current budget.

Review of budgets

Looking closely at the May ledger on the next pages (budget 1), notice that Associate is due on the 2nd; therefore, it was included in April's budget. The First Union is due the 1st; therefore, it was also saved in April. Likewise, the June First Union payment has been scheduled of 2 pay periods in May because there's not enough money ($550) in one paycheck to pay it. *I'll get a money order; fill in the information and save it until I have the whole payment. *The auto insurance was saved in April. Some of next's month's payments are also budgeted in 2 payments because there's not enough in one paycheck.

In the sample budget the $20.00 a week may not appear like much savings but it equals $80 a month. In six months, it's equal $480. In one year, it'll equal $960. Some financial agencies recommend that you set aside 10% of you earning towards savings, not a set amount, as used in our example. My recommendation is that you do the one that will motivate you to save, especially for retirement.

There are fewer savings in the May only budget (budget 2) because of late payment fees, but the goal of $80.00 for savings was reached. It may be wise to use the extra money to prepay a bill so that the debt is not increased by a late fee.

Discipline is a key factor in the following May budget.

1. Discipline to pay tithing and trust God to provide according to His Word.

2. Discipline to find free recreational/leisure activities until the next week.

3. Discipline to contribute toward the vision plan and savings.

budget ledger 1   May 0000

(remember "Pd" in April means money was saved in April to pay the amount due I May.)

parenthesis indicate due weekly or monthly

Pay dates			7	14	21	28	
Paycheck amount			$550	$550	$550	$550	

Duedate Pd	Bill/Balance	7 amt due	14 amt due	21 amt due	28 amt due
weekly	tithing	$55	$55	$55	$55
5-2 ($50)	Associates/1997.40	Pd in Apri			*$50
5-1 ($600)	First Union/ 60,000	Pd in Apr		*$300	*$300
5-18 ($38)	MasterCh /1350		$38		
5-1 ($200)	Allstate/200	Pd in April	*$100	*$100	
5-15 ($200)	Auto loan/ 9000.	$200----	----------	---------	--------
as plan	Groc/food/ varies	$125	$125		$75
weekly	Car gas/varies	$20	$20	$20	$20
5-30 ($100)	Electric		$100		
5-15 ($50)	Water	$50--	----------	---------	--------
5-10 ($75)	Heat	$75--	----------	---------	--------
weekly	Saving/ $80	$20	$20	$20	$20
Total Owed		$545.00	$458	$495	$520
+/-		+5	+92	+55	+30

*payments for upcoming bill in June
Utilities balances are left blank in the balance column in this budget because they are paid in full each month. For bills that are set up on a payment plan with a utility company, a balance amount would be placed in the balance space. If you did not pay the entire bill each month, the leftover balance would be placed in the balance space.

Budget ledger 2   May 0000
(All bills will be paid with May paycheck)

Pay dates	7	14	21	28
Paycheck amount	$550	$550	$550	$550

Duedate	Pd	Bill/Balance	7 amt due	14 amt due	21 amt due	28 amt due
weekly		tithing	$55	$55	$55	$55
5-2 ($50)		Associates 1997.40	$50			$!!20
5-1 ($600)		First Union/ 60,000	$300	*$330	(*no late fees	til the 17th
5-18 ($38)		MasterCh/ 1350			$38	$!!20
5-1($200)		Allstate /200				$200
5-15($200)		Auto loan/9000.		$75	$125--	-----------
as plan		Groc/food	$100	$100		$125
weekly		Car gas	$15	$15	$15	$15
5-30 ($100)		Electric			$100--	-----------
5-15($50)		Water			$50--	-----------
5-1($75)		Heat	$25		$50--	-----------
weekly		Saving $80			$50	$30------
Total Owed			$545.00	$545	$ 483	$465
+/-			+5	+5	+67	+85

<u>!!Indicates you incurred a late payment fee for the bill</u>

According to the example budgets, 1 and 2, we often have enough money to pay obligations, with some money left over to control. Without budgeting one could order pizza costing $20.00 when I really only have $5.00; or spend $10.00 at

McDonald's when I only have $5.00 to spend. I've spent an excess $15.00 with the pizza; or an excess $5.00 with the 10.00. I have actually squeezed into the wrong size and will feel the pain when I do not have enough money for necessities.

However, with budgeting I can move money around so that I can have more money in a given week or month. I am now in control of where and when money is spent. The longer I budget, the more control I gain.

The same method is followed if you are paid bi-weekly or once a month. Bi-weekly, the amount due will go under the date you will pay them according to your paycheck dates. for example all of the bills under the 7th would now be under the 14th. All of the bills under the 14th will be under the 28th if my only pay dates are the 14th and 28th.

If paid once a month all the bills can be paid at one time. Creative planning is required to ensure that there are no late fees. For example, planning to keep bills one month ahead will avoid late payments when paid twice or once a month. Just remember, not to send the payment off until it will be credited for the correct month. Keeping bills a month ahead can be accomplished by months of planning and discipline.

I've also included a column for the amount of interest that I pay each month. Keeping track of the interest encouraged me to pay a little more each month because I could see that I was giving the company 20.00 dollars each month. The mortgage interest made a big difference. I imagined all the things I could have done with that extra 240.00 per year.

You can also include column that indicates the amount of principal and the amount of interest that was applied to the bill. This will help you see as we discussed in Chapter III, how much the money is costing you; as well as, how much you are giving monthly and yearly to the companies.

For example, I write in a column that I paid $25 in interest $55.00; since, I can sacrifice and pay it. Eventually, I will pay off the bill sooner, and next month I should pay a few dollars less in interest.

Keeping Track of Receipts

Compare receipts with the money in your budget. Reviewing your receipts will help you see exactly where you spent chunks of your money; especially if an item was not included on your budget ledger page; such as, popcorn at the movie theatre. (Was that your emergency savings you spent on popcorn?☺)

There are apps and websites for receipt tracking also. Please research them to ensure they are valid and meet your needs. Your financial institution may also provide a receipt tracking ledger. You may find it tedious or time consuming to try to document every single item on the receipt. I've provided example pages with categories that you can check off to determine the type of items you spend most of your money on.

Chapter VII
I Don't Have Enough Money to Budget

I Don't Have Enough Money to Budget
I've read the Scriptures through and through
But I don't know what to do.
And I've heard from those of authority.
That, "God shall supply your every need,
According to His riches in glory."
Just trust in Him and you'll see,
He'll do for you what He's done for me!
But my debts are high and my bills are many.
I cannot keep a single penny.
Lord, Lord, what shall I do?

One of the main reasons some people refuse to budget is that they do not have 100% of moneys needed to pay bills each month. It is possible to start a budget without enough money to pay all your bills. In fact budgeting will change this situation if you endure long enough.

The procedure for budgeting without enough finances is the same; however, additional steps are needed. The first step involves attitude and honesty. First, honestly ask the questions, "Why do I not have enough money to pay all my bills?" "Is it because of late payment fees?" "Do I earn enough money to live at the standard I've chosen?" "Did an emergency occur?" etc. Once you know the cause, you can work on eliminating it, or getting your finances in order.

The second step is to contact businesses and recommit to payment. A phone call followed by a written note is appropriate. The written note will provide you with a paper trail and a vision of what you've decided. Often, a business will offer a repayment plan to lower payments. Remember lowering payments usually means paying more money over a longer period of time. Before requesting lower payments look for other ways to lower debt. Can you lower your utility or other household bills? Buy a less expensive vehicle or forego a desired item? The main point is to budget even when there appears to be a lack of money. It is the best way to get back in control of your finances. You will eliminate bills quicker and see more money in your pocket than if you continue without a budget

Caution: Dealing with creditors on phone and through letters

I found that creditors consistently wrote or said nice things to get the response they wanted from me. They often tried to convince me that I had money that I really didn't have, or at least not liquid cash. Here is a scenario of what actually happened when I responded·to a letter stating, "call us we can work with you, we have something that can help you" on an account that was paid 45 days late.
(Rep) "This account is seriously past due. We must have $250 in our office by this p.m." *notice-no mention of we can work with you on this* If you

do a phone check, we can take care of this right now. I can offer an extension on the other $250". When I refused to do a phone check we got into a heated debated conversation ending with, "If I had $250 to send you today, I wouldn't be in this predicament."

(Rep) "We have not received Oct, Nov payments. You are seriously delinquent in this obligation, and we need $250 today." (Me) "I'm aware of that and calling to acknowledge and verify that a payment has been mailed."

(Rep) "What amount was mailed?"

(Me) Check #206 in the amount of $250 was mailed on Nov 11th. ."

(Rep) "That amount does not cover your obligation. We need $250 today on this account."

(Me) "I didn't call you today to bicker about a payment. GOODBYE!"

The point is when calling creditors; remember that their goal is to get money for the company. Do not be discouraged when they do not appear as pleasant and kind as their initial letters. Commit to fulfill your obligation to them anyway.

I often wondered if creditors think that there are people who have money stashed(maybe under their mattresses☺) and are simply refusing to pay their utility bills. Or, maybe the average person plays a game of toss up the bill and pay the one that falls first, or pay the person who convinces me that I have what I don't have, or who's best at harassing.

I once asked a representative why they continued to call me several times a day; even though I'd made the payments and arrangements to pay the past due amount. I was told that my name would stay in a data base until the past due payment was received.

The best approach to not having enough money is to face the situation honestly. If you're budgeting and really trying to pay off debts continue to pay, while finding ways to eliminate debt.

Keep a determined positive attitude. Do not become discouraged by the lack of funding during this season in your life.

What do you do while getting your finances in order? Bill collectors are calling!

There's not enough money for recreation. You feel like you work each day, so another you can pay!

1. Remember the Christian principal of budgeting: "a wicked man borrowed and payeth not again.

2. Respond to continued calls with written acknowledgement of them.

3. Acknowledge phone calls honestly but do not be discouraged by the lack of empathy from creditors. After all, his/her job is to get money for the company. If you feel that you are being harassed, call the consumer bureau in your state and report it. Being honest and realistic means, if you can only pay $10, do not be pressured into saying "I'll send

$20.00. You know from your budget how much you can really pay.

4. Request a free copy of your credit report from freeannualreport.com

Credit counseling is wonderful if it is free. There is no such thing as eliminating bad credit "quickly" if you have not paid your bills on time. Credit repair is accomplished in two ways:

1. Start and continue to pay debt as contracted (on time).

2. After a specific number of years (usually seven*) credit reports will no longer reflect bill history for bills paid in full. *seven years from the date of last bill activity or payment in full.

There are numerous credit agencies that will work with creditors for you for a fee. It is advisable to research any company you would like to get help from. Find out what the company will do for you; how much it will cost you; does the better business bureau have information on the company. Get a written contract from the company that explains what you are to do and what the company will do.

Credit counseling companies will often contact the companies and set up payment plans for you. You can do this for yourself if you have the time, patience, and tolerance to discuss your obligations with the creditors. Usually there are stipulations on the type of credit counseling the company will help you with. Collateral related credit; such as mortgages are usually excluded. There are companies that will contact your mortgage company to rearrange payments. Again, usually you can do this yourself with patience, persistence, tolerance, copy of your credit report and bill statement.

For example, for fifty dollars a month, the counseling agency may contact creditors, request lower interest rates and arrange a payment plan to fit an amount you and the counseling agency agreed would be feasible. Each month, the total needed plus the fifty dollar fee is sent to the counseling company. The company disperses to the agencies the amount that you and the company agreed in the contract would be paid.

Many financial organizations; such as, credit unions and banks offer free credit counseling. They provide the financial information needed about your finances. You then put this information into action; for example, setting up the budget, contacting the companies to lower interest rates, payments.

Eliminate loans and credits cards that keep you owing them. Cut and return high interest credit cards with a written note to close the account. Try to use cash more. The more cash you spend, the sooner you'll see the actual cost of items. Also you won't pay extra money in fees and interest.

If you have a bank "debit" card that can be used in places where Visa or Master Charge are accepted, you can use it without the interest fees. Be aware of the stipulations by different agencies when planning to use the card instead of a Visa or Master Charge. For example, at a car rental company, how much extra will be on hold until you return the vehicle; how long it take the bank to release this hold. Using a debit card requires dedication in keeping track of moneys used. The amount used is not always immediately debited from your account; therefore, your balance may be reflected incorrectly. On the other hand, using your bank card for major reservations may cause your account to be frozen at the amount placed on your card stays on the card as long as 4 to 5 days after you have paid for it. In short, the amount that you authorized for the rental reservations will not be available for other use unless you are allowed to use cash at the time of the transaction instead of the debit card; even though, you made reservation with it. For example, you rent a vehicle for 3 days for two hundred thirty five dollars, and made hotel reservations for one hundred and five dollars on your debit card.

The rental company placed an additional two hundred dollars on the bankcard as security for a total of five hundred and forty dollars. When you paid cash for the hotel, seventy five dollars were never process; therefore, it was available immediately. When you returned the rental vehicle, you paid with your bankcard but the transaction did not actually process for 3 days later. On the fourth day, the two hundred dollars is credited back to your account. You'll probably notice a disclaimer that indicates that the company cannot guarantee the date that the money is credited back by your bank.

The advantage is you did not pay user fees or interest. The disadvantage is you had to preplan for moneys you would need from your account. You also had to keep track of everything to avoid having transactions denied when using the balance left on the card.

Peer Pressure?? Do you believe that adults experience peer pressure? It appears that a lack of discipline and the pride of life contribute to adult peer pressure. There is good pride and not so good pride. Pride has several definitions according to Webster. Definitions range from "exaggerated self-esteem; conceit; proper respect for oneself"; to "delight or satisfaction in one's own achievements". It is the "exaggerated" that gets us into debt trouble. Solomon taught in Proverbs 13:10 that "only by pride cometh contention:"…
It is this type of pride that will prevent us from saying "no I can't go out to eat with you today."

We determine the level of pride, where pride is needed and what to apply it to.

As you get your finances in order, do not allow pride to get in the way.

Stay focused on your vision plan.

Computer generated programs; such as, Quicken, or budget simple are great for budgeting if you already have a computer; a reliable program and know how to use it. Buying a computer and software may not help you save more money if you do not put the other aspects of budgeting in place.

There are many wonderful electronic programs to explore. These programs help with the math, tracking, and are time savers, but remember budgeting through God's Word is more than figures. It's about discipline, and wisdom, and attitude.

Attitude is mentioned here; because a disciplined, positive attitude and persistence, is required in order to be successful in budgeting.

The internet or your financial institution is a great place to explore electronic budgets. However, I warn that as you become accustomed to getting the math done for you via an electronic program, do not lose the essence of budgeting explained in the previous chapters. Okay, you are confident that you will benefit from an electronic program. You really want to try those budget apps, coupon apps, other apps. I recommend that you explore your options.

Determine what type of program/app you need, for example:

-Budgeting only
-Investment tracking
-Connection to other financial institutions

Determine the cost of the program or app and where it fits in your budget. (Be mindful that "free" may not mean free forever, or "basic" or "standard" may be a strategy to entice you to purchase a costly, "premium program".

I've researched a few, but I cannot make any recommendations because your budget is a personal financial matter. I recommend you start with creating the budget manual as indicated in the previous chapter; even if only once.

The sites I was curious enough to research are budgetsimple.com; Feedthepig.org; Bankrate.com

Mint.com; My spending plan, Money tracking.
Helpful sites I've seen in material I read are:
ebates.com, shopathome.com, southersavers.com,
befrugal.com.
Yes, I like Apps that I can download and use while
out shopping. No comments on any sites or apps
because you must do your own research and decide
if this is for you, keeping in mind the information
from other parts of this book☺.

Chapter VIII
Budgeting With a Spouse

Research shows that finances directly affect marriages.

Through budgeting we can learn that as married couples we have an advantage because the word says: "And they twain shall be one flesh: so they are no more twain, but one flesh. (Mark 10:8) For where two or three are gathered together in my name, there am I in the midst of them. ..." (Matthew 18:20)

I don't say "my other half" when it comes a marriage. People tend to visualize half of 100. We should be 100% when we enter into a relationship because God does not create partial things. Sometimes we may need to provide 60% because the other person can only give 40%. How can we give 60% if we are only 50%?

We enter into marriage 100% + 100% equaling a 200% relationship. Therefore in budgeting, I encourage both spouses to be involved.

It is difficult to share the responsibility for anything without all parties being actively involved. Each person must accept the responsibility for a part of the finances whether through moneys from a paycheck or being responsible with items that affect the finances.

The responsibilities and expectations of finances should be discussed prior to marriage. Expectations and habits should be addressed. How money will be spent should be addressed under such topics as hobbies; recreation, housing, children, furniture, clothing, health, personal hygiene, etc.

Okay, so you're already married and you didn't discuss these topics prior. In fact you've been married for many years but never stopped to talk about them. NOW IS THE TIME☺!

Integrity

Before we go any further, let's talk about integrity. We are going to use Webster's integrity definition of "quality or state of being of sound moral principal; uprightness, honestly, and sincerity." Integrity must be defined here, because the information in this section is based on integrity in a relationship. It's good to agree to a plan but not keeping your word by doing it, destroys the plan.

Communication, commitment and compassion are also basic three "Cs" for any relationship: marriage, family or friendships. These should be already in the relationship prior to confronting issues with budgeting.

So you've been married for years and haven't stopped to discuss any of the financial topics; specifically budgeting.

1. Start at the beginning by taking a stand on issues that affect your budget.

2. What is the issue at hand? What concerns you about keeping track of finances in your household?

3. What is the best way and time to approach your spouse about your concerns?

4. Know how you'd like to resolve the issue, but realize that your spouse may have a better plan.

5. Try to end the conversation with some type of resolution. Otherwise you'll feel that the conversation was in vain or didn't communicate what was intended.

There are many questions that arise with marriage and finances. Many of the questions and answers are unique to each individual marriage. How they are answered depends on the marriage. Therefore, answers to questions are not directly addressed in this chapter. Questions that may arise include:
How do I get my spouse to share paycheck amounts with me?
How do I get my spouse to stop spending money on people outside our household?
How do we change our spending attitude?
My spouse never buys anything. All the money is in the bank. We are misers. What do I do?
How do we agree on where to invest the budget savings?

If you cannot resolve these concerns among yourselves, find a reputable professional; such as a financial advisor or counselor, to help resolve the situation. Resolving disagreements will help you move forward with budgeting.

My husband and I have been married 30+ years. We started out with separate accounts because we already had accounts in 2 different states when we were married. We established joint accounts so that either of us could use them. We used our accounts as if they were separate accounts. We communicated to each other when we used money from the other's account. We kept separate bills prior to having an official budget, but we depended on each other if we needed extra money. We knew each other's pay dates and paycheck amounts. I informed him if I needed to go into his primary account. He informed me also if he withdrew money from my primary account. A simple, "I need to take one hundred dollars out of the account" sufficed for us. We switched bills when we found it more beneficial. For example, if my paycheck amount and pay dates allowed me to schedule a bill on my ledger that was more beneficial than on his, we switch. Switching allows us to avoid late fees, and other frustrations. At times, one of us would take on an extra bill to ensure it was paid. We keep separate ledgers because our record keeping styles are different and our lives were so busy that it was easier to keep track of our own ledgers.

Using budgeting in our marriage eliminated many frustrations; allowed us to move forward with joint and individual visions, and gave us knowledge of what to specifically pray and fast about.

Yes sometimes we had financial difficulties. But they were easier to avoid or overcome because we knew "how much", "where", and "when" about money coming in into our family.

Chapter IX
Just My Opinion
Desperate Times Require Desperate Measures!

I may be incorrect in this opinion, but: the past housing market had many families in an uproar. It has brought to the forefront practices that have been going on for years in the lending business, and still are to some degree. This practice, that is now called subprime lending and predatory lending, was not uncommon and depicted in many old movies; ; wherein, we see money loaned to persons in need with outstanding interest and fees. This basically happened to the poor, disadvantages or specific races of people.

Predatory lending was morally wrong, but so is an Alcohol Beverage Store or internet gambling casino in the middle of a low income, high unemployment neighborhood, which inevitable encourages the increase in the purchases of alcoholic beverages and gambling at a time when people are trying to seek out hope.

(I do not mean to sound ludicrous), but at least predatory lending and subprime lending indirectly gave the people the experience of owning a home and paying property taxes, unlike alcoholic beverages and gambling which is destructive to families without any meaningful consequences.

If the subprime lenders had been smart, they would have set up a support system to assist the borrowers; much like the government does with an addiction program for alcohol and drugs after stores are conveniently placed. Instead, these lenders often resold the loans to companies that were less sympathetic, increased the fees and refused to try to assist the borrowers.

Is it true that the people simply could not repay the loans? It's only partially true. They could have repaid with two things happening. One is budget disciplining; the other, the company lowering the payments until such time that the economy became more stable.

There are other situations similar to subprime lending and pay day loans. It is food deserts, gas gauging, high insurance rates, and lack of cost of living raises. Eventually, we will begin to see medical bills from poor food choices over take the income of many. We won't pay one hundred percent in interest, but one hundred percent in nutritional value, etc., is taken away from those who need it the most.

Budget discipline in these situations is very important. Is it more important to purchase bling, shoes, cars, etc. or pay more on the mortgage and buy healthier foods? Without the budget, we gave all our money away without knowing we'd suddenly need it when the lender decided that we were no longer credit worthy and would not re-finance the loans at a lower rate.

I also say it is only partially true because with budgeting, the mortgage and finance situations would have had a different result if the economy had not changed negatively. Salaries did not keep up with the cost of living.

Homeowners made purchases of vehicles and houses based on normal salary increases in our society. In short, each year we anticipate a salary increase. However, unemployment increased. The cost of health insurance soared. The cost of fuel became excessive. Unlike what was typical in our society, salaries were not adequate enough to keep up with typical living costs. Also, the value of homes did not increase as they had in the past.

Instead of mortgage companies recognizing and sympathizing with this, they attempted to squeeze blood from the turnip. Unfortunately there was no blood in the turnip.

These companies became less sympathetic and more militant. They decide to use foreclosure as a weapon. Before they realized what they were doing, they'd driven down the value of homes and the value of the concept of homeownership; thereby hurting themselves and society.

So what's a person to do in times like these? Desperate times require desperate measures?

First do you have your vision plan in place? Do you have budget discipline?

Ask "How am I going to keep up the mortgage payments?" "How am I going to eat healthy?" "How important is this?" What type of changes need to be made in the household to ensure money is available for mortgage, healthy living, etc.?

Some people resorted to filing bankruptcy. That's a decision to discuss with a bankruptcy attorney, and weigh the personal cost before making that decision.

Refinancing to a lower rate would be the ideal option for a mortgage loan and trying to pay it off.

Finding ways for extra money is not easy, but traditional ways may work; such as, taking on a renter, or working an extra job until you can get back on stable ground.

Chapter X
Finding Money in Your Budget

1--At the top of my list for finding money is "couponing". Couponing is like sweat equity when buying a house. The more work you do to save money, the more of your own money you will have. Couponing requires planning and organization. You must determine a few things:

--What types of coupons will you clip: groceries/household, restaurant, clothing sales, etc.?

--How much money will you spend on acquiring coupons? Ensure you are getting the money back that you spend getting coupons from newspapers, magazines, websites, etc.

--What type of organizer will you use: a notebook system, a coupon pocket, or Apps?

--When will you sit down to determine needed coupons, and clip the coupons, or send them to your app?

--Who is available to assist you? Family, friends, coupon clubs, etc.

2--Take advantage of store points and reward cards for additional groceries, or gas.

3--Take advantage of special shopping days provided because of your age, military service, etc.

4-- Get reimbursed for recycling cans and bottles if you live in an area that allows you to return them for 5 cents, etc.

5--Take advantage of websites that offer rebates after carefully researching them. Only use them when you need items from the website. Wait until you can order more than one item and get a bigger rebate check back.

6--Plan your menus. Plan your menus around what you have in the cupboard and freezer from couponing, or, plan your menu around sale items for that week. For example, if you want a pork chop meal, plan it the week that pork chops are on sale. Veggie and fruit are seasonal items; therefore, you'll save money if your menu matches what's in season.

7--Garden-If you have the space, a few tomato plants can save valuable dollars; instead of, buying them at the grocery store all summer. If possible join the community gardening space club. Can you have a patio container garden? I've been told by a gardener to put extra seeds in the freezer for the next year. You can share extra seeds with a friend or neighbor.

8--Technology has made saving money and couponing much easier. Research sites; such as southernsavers.com that will assist you with coupon and store specials. You can also join online savings clubs for groceries and other items.

9—When pumping gas, stop the pump before reaching the whole dollar amount to avoid going over the planned amount It's much easier to stop between $29.90 and $ 29.99 then exactly on $30.00.

10—Find family or friends who're willing to buy in bulk with you, split the cost and the items. Some wholesale bulk clubs even allow you to combine their coupons with the manufacturer's coupons.

11—Re-gifting and Thrift store gifting.

- Did you know that Re-Gifting is generally an acceptable practice
- Wiki says it best:
  "National Regifting Day is an annual observance held each year on the Thursday before Christmas. Many office holiday parties are held on this day, and research shows that 40 percent of office party gifts are re-gifted—that is, something given to someone and then re-given to another person without use".-quoted from http://en.wikipedia.org/wiki/National_Regifting_Day

- **When Re-gifting:**
  - ♦ Look for items that contain their original containers, packages, booklets, etc
  - ♦ Look for New and Unused items; even if they've been opened
  - ♦ **The gift should be unwrapped and rewrapped: *It's a gift from you, not the previous giver**
  - ♦ **Re-gift items that the receiver can use and really wants; not just to get it out of your possession ☺(unless it's a gag gift, of course)**
- Never re-gift in the circle that the gift was received in; as this may be offensive to some people.
- ******Find more info on Re-gifting popularity on the web.******

Remember every seed planted requires time to sprout in the ground, and then grow into a small plant, then flower, then produce its fruit. If anything stops the process, it will never bear its fruit. So it is with budgeting.

Acknowledgement of Works cited within this publication

Dave Branon, *Our Daily Bread®,* © 1997 by RBC Ministries, Grand Rapids, MI. Reprinted by permission. All rights reserved.

Webster's New World Dictionary of American English, 3rd ed. (1994), s.v. "rebuke"; "vision"; "pride"; "integrity".

W.E.Vines. Vines Expository Dictionary of New Testament Words. s.v. "vision" MACDONALD Publishing Company

Bishop Don Meares, Dare to Be A Line Crosser. Pt 2, Evangel Church Media Ministry, Upper Marlboro, MD 16 Mar. 1997.

The Zonedervan Corporation. The Comparative Study Bible. Michigan 1984.

http://en.wikipedia.org/wiki/National_Regifting_Day

Use these tables to practice

Pay dates
Paycheck amount $ $ $ $

Bill/due	Pd	Bill Balance	amt due	amt due	amt due	amt due

Pay dates

Paycheck amount $ $ $ $

Bill/due date	Pd	Bill	Balance	interest	amt due	amt due	pd on

Pay dates _____

Paycheck amount | $ _____ | $ _____ | $ _____ | $ _____

Bill/due date	Pd	Bill	Balance	interest	amt due	amt due	pd on

Paycheck amount $_____ $_____ $_____ $_____

Bill/due date	Pd	Bill Balance	amt due	amt due	amt due	amt due

Paycheck amount $ $ $ $

Bill/due date	Pd	Bill Balance	amt due	amt due	amt due	amt due

Store/Restaurant _____

Total Receipt amount: _____

Categories

Grocery	Medical	Laundry	Snacks	Cleaning	Auto	Etc	Etc.

Store/Restaurant _____

Total Receipt amount: _____

Categories

Grocery	Medical	Laundry	Snacks	Cleaning	Auto	Etc	Etc.

Store/Restaurant _____

Total Receipt amount: _____

Categories

Grocery	Medical	Laundry	Snacks	Cleaning	Auto	Etc	Etc.

<u>Receipts List of Purchase</u>   <u>Receipt Total:</u>

　　　List all items purchased (clothing, medicines, tickets, snacks, groceries in groups); i.e. list all similar items together. Again if this is tedious, list by categories and put checks. For example instead of listing sugar, flour, chicken, hot dogs, write in Groceries and put four checks if you only bought four grocery items.

Store Name   Items

_____   _____   _____

_____   _____

_____   _____

_____   _____

_____   _____

_____   _____

_____   _____

_____   _____

Store Name   Items

_____   _____   _____

_____   _____

_____   _____

_____   _____

_____   _____

_____   _____

_____   _____

Store Name

Items

_____

_____   _____
_____   _____
_____   _____
_____   _____
_____   _____
_____   _____
_____   _____
_____   _____

Store Name

Items

_____

_____   _____
_____   _____
_____   _____
_____   _____
_____   _____
_____   _____
_____   _____
_____   _____

Store Name

Items

_____

_____   _____
_____   _____
_____   _____
_____   _____
_____   _____
_____   _____
_____   _____
_____   _____